A Merry Life, And a Short One

Unhelpful Self-Help and Terrible Advice
from the Golden Age of Piracy

Matt McLaine

D1362090

ISBN 978-1-795-67572-7

DEDICATION

To this vile Crew you may the Pyrate add,
Who puts to Sea the Merchant to invade,
And reaps the Profit of another's Trade.
He sculks behind some Rock, or swiftly flies
From Creek to Creek, rich Vessels to surprize.
By this ungodly Course the Robber gains,
And lays up so much Wealth, that he disdains
And mocks the poor, unprofitable toil
Of those, who plant the Vine, or till the Soil.
    - from "A Paraphrase on the Book of Job" by Sir Richard Blackmore (1700).

This book is dedicated to my wife and daughter, who have looted my heart.

PREFACE

Let's be clear: pirates were neither Robin Hood nor chivalrous liberators
nor loveable rogues. They were at best thieves and scoundrels, and too
often murderers, slavers, and worse. Of all the questionable advice you're
about to receive, here's the best you're likely to get: don't try any of these at
home! Or at sea, if you're so inclined. Of course, if you somehow acquire a
time machine and find yourself aboard ship in the early 18th century, give it
a whirl! You'll fit right in.

As pirate William Fly probably thought but never said, "There's a noose for
that."

Many quotes you'll find herein come from period sources. Where possible I
retained period spelling and capitalization, with generous editing to make
them readable to modern eyes. Several interior illustrations are taken from
Howard Pyle's "Book of Pirates," a collection of Pyle's late 19th and early
20th century stories and artwork, published posthumously in 1921.
Additional art was taken from Charles Ellms' 1821 work "The Pirates Own
Book," as well as various other public-domain sources.

Matt McLaine

INTRODUCTION

"A merry life and a short one shall be my motto." - Bartholomew Roberts

Spurred by politics, religion, wars at home in Europe, and mostly good old fashioned greed, pirates plagued the oceans throughout the late 17th and early 18th centuries. Early on, most European pirates - more properly, buccaneers - generally confined their raids to Spanish interests in the Americas. Poorly-guarded gold and silver does have a certain lure for greedy corsairs. Once England, France, the Netherlands, and Spain turned on one another in any one of half a dozen Continental wars, pirates gleefully followed suit, kicking off the Golden Age of Piracy. How long it lasted depends on whom you ask; 1688 to 1726 is as good an estimate as any. None of them made prisoners walk the plank and almost none actually buried treasure. There were a few female pirates, and a few black pirates, and quite a few people who wished they'd never heard of pirates. Pirates were legendary drinkers and loved few things more than converting their gold into as much alcohol as they could carry. They partied with other pirates, and groups of them would occasionally sail together too, fellow pirates being one of the few targets they almost never attacked. When their cannons roared, it was generally to scare a passing merchantman - pirates weren't looking for a fight, and sinking a target meant sinking its riches, which was like sinking potential rum. Worse still if the target were actually hauling brandy, wine, and other essentials, since pirates spent months at sea and often had to rely on capturing food and drink, their own food supplies usually having rotted shortly after leaving port. Not that moldy water or a few weevils in the biscuits would stop a hungry pirate. If you were captured by pirates and had a useful skill - navigation, carpentry, surgery, gunnery, rum-punch-making - chances were good they'd offer you a place in their crew, though you might end up "volunteering" at sword-point. If you did join, there were rules: the Pirate Code was real enough, and once you signed their Articles, every sailor from the Captain to the rat-catcher was bound equally. Pirates unlucky enough to be caught may face trial, and would be harangued by merchants seeking revenge, judges eager for justice, and ministers hoping to save a soul. They might not have had any good advice for the doomed pirates (though pirates awaiting execution sometimes had choice advice for their captors), but with luck - and possibly rum - perhaps our reader might find a nugget of wisdom amongst the fool's gold following.

A FURTHER VOYAGE

Throughout the text, watch for these
Further Voyage notes. Each features
freebooter facts and buccaneer bonuses,
with a distinct lack of atrocious advice.

Matt McLaine

PART ONE:

FRIENDS AND LOVERS

1: DON'T KEEP TOXIC PEOPLE IN YOUR LIFE

You've tried your best to work things out. You gave them time, tried to be understanding, and thought back to all the great times you had together. Unfortunately sometimes it's not enough. No matter how close you may have been as friends, when they're bringing down themselves and everyone nearby, when they've turned cruel or bitter, when they refuse all help, sometimes you have to let them go. There comes a time when you have to think about yourself and your own mental health, and that time is now.

Charles Vane was a firebrand of a pirate. When England offered a pardon to all pirates who surrendered by late 1718, hundreds accepted. Vane refused and shot his way out of port in a blaze of glory before going on a piratical looting spree. His moment of stardom lasted until his courage failed him the moment he faced a real challenge, a moment his crew would neither forget nor forgive.

"[T]he latter end of November; they then fell in with a ship, which it was expected would have struck as soon as their black colors were hoisted; but instead of this she discharged a broadside upon the pirate, and hoisted French colors, which showed her to be a French man-of-war. ... During this chase the pirates were divided in their resolution what to do. Vane, the captain, was for making off as fast as he could, alleging that the man-of-war was too strong for them to cope with ... the next day, the captain's conduct was obliged to stand

3

the test of a vote, and a resolution passed against his honor and dignity, which branded him with the name of coward, deposed him from the command, and turned him out of the company with marks of infamy."
- Charles Ellms, "The Pirates Own Book" (1837)

Vane's own crewmen weren't the first or last to get tired of his grandstanding. He even tried convincing the legendary Blackbeard to sail with him! They partied together for days but in the end Blackbeard declined and sent Vane on his way. Vane should have seen the writing on the wall and changed his ways; his crew certainly didn't miss the signs.

A FURTHER VOYAGE

The pirate who called a vote to oust Vane from command was John "Calico Jack" Rackham. He was not particularly successful but became better known for two of his sailors: female pirates Mary Reed and Anne Bonny.

2: KNOW WHEN YOU HAVE A GOOD THING

Friends driving you bonkers with little quirks and annoyances? They're only human, and they probably see you the same way. True friendship is stronger than the little trials of life. Even a serious disagreement can be overcome with the kind of well-tested patience and deep understanding which comes from a friendship built on trust.

John Halsey had been a privateer in British service in 1701, sailing against the French and Spanish. By 1706 he had turned to piracy, sailing for the Indian Ocean by way of Madagascar. Despite Halsey's admirable record, his crew mistook his conscience for cowardice and deposed him before attacking the biggest ship they could find. They quickly found that they'd bitten off more than they could chew, and that removing an experienced and successful leader might not have been wise.

"He then sailed to the Red Sea, another happy hunting ground of the pirates, and met a big Dutch ship armed with sixty guns. Halsey astounded his men by announcing his sudden determination to attack only Moorish ships in the future. The indignant crew mutinied, threw Captain Halsey and his chief gunner in irons, and proceeded to attack the Dutchman. The mutinous pirates got the worst of the encounter, and released Halsey, who only just managed to get his ship away."
- Philip Gosse, "The Pirates' Who's Who" (1924)

Halsey led them to great riches over the next two years. Whether the crew came begging him to take command once more or not, they never again rose in mutiny. Too bad for them their ship was nearly shattered before they learned their lesson.

A FURTHER VOYAGE

In 1705 on Madagascar Halsey picked up castaways from the lost ship *Degrave*. Among the *Degrave* survivors were the son of Admiral John Benbow, as well as Robert Drury, who penned a popular memoir.

3: KNOW YOUR TARGET AUDIENCE

Even among friends there are limits. Jokes can go too far and feelings can get hurt by careless comments and unintended insults. The key to preventing this is to remember why you're friends in the first place. What brought you together? What shared experiences, laughs, and trials have kept you together?

William Moody and his 130-man crew had great success capturing merchant ships in 1718 and 1719. Some he merely looted; others he burned or sank, setting their crews adrift on the ocean in tiny boats with few supplies. When a sailor named Thomas Cocklyn tried to start a mutiny off the coast of Africa, Moody stranded Cocklyn and his supporters ashore and kept their shares of treasure. Moody's crew resented his treatment of Cocklyn and gave Moody a taste of his own medicine, setting him and his officers adrift before returning to join up with Cocklyn and the others.

"This Cocklyn and his men were truly a set of the basest and most cruel villains ever known. The united companies chose Cocklyn for their commander because of his brutality, being determined they said, never again to have a gentleman commander such as Moody was."
 - Charles Grey, "Pirates of the Eastern Seas" (1933)

Moody stole from, burned, and marooned his targets, and wasn't above abandoning his own sailors to steal their loot, and his crew *still* turned on him for being too nice! Now *that's* failure to appreciate what brought his crew together.

4: KEEP YOUR FRIENDS CLOSE

Friends help one another when the need is genuine. They stick together through thick and thin; fair-weather friends are no friends at all, while silence and abandonment are the surest signs that a supposed friend - isn't. Whether it's a helping hand or an encouraging word, when your friends need you, be there for them, and if they're true, they'll return the favor.

Edward Low and Charles Harris served together under the villainous pirate George Lowther in 1722. They soon left to sail on their own, trading ships back and forth throughout the Caribbean and the Americas. But when in 1723 Low mistook the British warship *Greyhound* for a whaling vessel, it was his erstwhile friend Harris who would pay the price.

"Captain Peter Solgard of the *Greyhound* then concentrated his fire on the sloop commanded by Harris, allowing Low to escape. Shot after shot raked buccaneer Harris' craft. The mainsail was first to fall, after which the sloop was gradually reduced to a helpless hulk. At four o'clock Captain Harris saw that further fighting was useless and surrendered, asking for quarter. One pirate suggested that they all blow themselves up, but Harris refused this solution of their troubles, whereupon the pirate committed suicide. An hour later all the pirates had been brought aboard the Greyhound as prisoners, and the pursuit of Captain Low began. Darkness fell before the man-of-war could overtake Low, so once again this villain succeeded in making

good his escape."
- Edward Rowe Snow, "Pirates and Buccaneers of the Atlantic Coast" (1944)

Low - already one of the most brutal and sadistic of the Golden Age pirates - was said to have become even more so afterwards, in anger over Harris' capture and death. If he cared about Harris so much, maybe he shouldn't have turned tail and run at the first sign of trouble!

A FURTHER VOYAGE

Harris and twenty-five other pirates were hanged in July 1723; to this day it remains the largest mass execution in Rhode Island History. Reverend Cotton Mather, famed from the Salem witch trials, preached to the condemned pirates.

5: IF YOU CAN'T BEAT 'EM, JOIN 'EM

Friends can be found in the strangest places, and a shared conflict - even from opposite sides - can bring people together in the oddest ways. If you keep your eyes (and options) open, you might find companions, forgiveness, assistance, and even honest employment where you least expect it, weren't looking for it, or didn't deserve it.

Benjamin Hornigold was a legendary pirate in the Caribbean, one of the most respected leaders of the "Flying Gang" who ruled the Bahamas in the early 18th century. When he saw the days of easy piracy were coming to an end, he not only accepted a pardon but enthusiastically offered his services to the new Governor as a pirate-hunter.

"So the said Captains Hornigold and Cockram set Sail that Night, and in three or four Days after took the Sloop *Woolfe*, Nicholas Woodall, Master, that had traded with Charles Vane, the Pyrate, and carried him to his Excellency the Governor of Providence, who seized his Vessel, and consined him Prisoner. "
- Charles Johnson, "A General History of the Pyrates, Volume 2."
(1724)

Intercepting the smuggler Woodall wasn't the only time Hornigold turned on his old pirate comrades who'd refused to see the light. Governor Woodes Rogers later wrote that Hornigold and Cockram "by their behaviour since my arrival gave me full confidence of their sincerity. ... I am glad of this new proof Capt. Hornigold has given the world to wipe off the infamous name he has hitherto been known by." High praise from the man sent by the English Crown to stamp out piracy in the Bahamas!

6: TREAT YOUR FRIENDS WELL

Friendship is an equal partnership of trust. Generosity without expecting reward is its hallmark, and apology for offenses should be offered without being asked. When that bond of equality changes from partners to givers versus takers, the friendship is living on borrowed time.

When Charles Vane stormed out of Nassau, he stole Charles Yeats' sloop to do so. Before Vane's own crew ejected him for cowardice, he'd granted Yeats command of a captured ship and sailed together for a time, but he used Yeats' ship as a floating storehouse. Yeats, finally fed up with Vane treating him as a subordinate - and with Vane's refusal to attack rich but risky targets - stole their latest haul and sailed to Charleston to seek a pardon.

"For Captain Vane, having always treated his Consort with very little Respect, assuming a Superiority over Yeats and his small Crew, and regarding the Vessel but as a Tender to his own; gave them a Disgust, who thought themselves as good Pyrates, and as great Rogues as the best of them; so they caball'd together, and resolved to take the first Opportunity to leave the Company; and accept of his Majesty's Pardon, or set up for themselves, either of which they thought more honourable than to be Servants to the former..."
- Charles Johnson, "A General History of the Pyrates." (1724)

Even though Vane restarted his piracy by hijacking Yeats' own vessel - and attacking a fellow pirate was something rarely done and near universally disliked - Yeats might still have forgiven him. They had success together, capturing ships and claiming loot, but Vane couldn't see past his own ego. Vane lost half his fleet and some of his most valuable treasure by pushing Yeats too far. If only he'd made amends with Yeats and treated him as an equal and a partner, Vane might have been more than a footnote to piracy's Golden Age.

7: DO ANYTHING FOR LOVE

Ah, love! When your heart beats for that special someone, you know you'll go to almost any lengths for them. Your happiness and theirs are intertwined. Share risks and hardships together, and you'll have shared joys and shared rewards as your prize. If either party isn't willing to put in effort for the relationship, then is it truly love?

John Bear's loyalties were fickle: he first served the English, then the Spanish, and finally the French, traveling to whichever island would condone his piracy with a wink and a nod. When it came to love, though, he went out of his way to elope with pirate style and pull off a suitably dashing (and devious) wedding.

"[August 1687: A letter from] Lieutenant Governor Molesworth to William Blathwayt: ... [Captain] Spragge told me that he heard from Campeachy that Bear was married at Havanna, and gave himself out as a faithful subject of the King of Spain. I have therefore sent Captain Spragge to Havanna to demand him as a pirate and an English subject. He gave out that his wife was a noblewoman, who ran away with him, and they actually fired the guns of the Castle as a salute to her, while the Governor and most of the chief men of the town were present at the wedding."
- J. W. Fortescue, "Calendar of State Papers Colonial, America and West Indies: Volume 12" (1899)

Jamaican Governor Hender Molesworth went on to write, "The nobleman's daughter is a strumpet that he used to carry with him in man's apparel, and is the daughter of a rum-punch-woman of Port Royal." Bear not only convinced the Governor of Havana that his "strumpet" was a proper lady of high society, but was willing to smuggle her out of Jamaica dressed as a man! He may have been a pirate and a rogue, and she may have been a moonshiner's daughter, but it was clearly a match made in heaven.

8: FRIENDS IN HIGH PLACES

Sometimes it's not what you know, it's who you know. Cultivate a wide circle of friends - network! - and know who can help you when you're in a tight situation. Don't be afraid to ask for help, either - those in a position to provide assistance will often do so gladly, knowing you'll return the favor.

Though he was English, even fellow Englishmen weren't safe from pirate George Bond. In the early 1680's he looted English, Dutch, and French ships without fear. What made him so bold was his patronage by Adolph Esmit, the Danish Governor of St. Thomas. Esmit paid Bond and his crew to bring in ships, hid the ships from angry foreign governments by pretending Bond had found them adrift, and more.

"[A letter from] Sir William Stapleton to Lords of Trade and Plantations: Having received frequent complaints of the villainy of the Governor of St. Thomas, I beseech you to read the annexed depositions, and, if you think fit, to move His Majesty to ask satisfaction against the King of Denmark's Governor for fitting out a pirate, George Bond, receiving his captures, and protecting all the robbers ... My lords, there is no safe trading to or from these parts until that receptacle of thieves and sea-robbers be reduced or that Governor hanged who so openly protects them."
- J. W. Fortescue, "Calendar of State Papers Colonial, America and West Indies: Volume 11" (1898)

Bond wasn't the only pirate Esmit protected: he had offered similar services to French corsair Jean Hamlin, among others. Esmit himself must have had similarly highly-placed friends: he was removed from office more than once for corruption but always seemed to avoid prosecution, much like his pirate allies.

PART TWO:

BLUSTER AND BRAVADO

9: IF YOU CAN'T DAZZLE THEM WITH BRILLIANCE, BAFFLE THEM WITH BULL

Honesty may be the best policy but when everything is on the line - sustenance, security, even survival - be prepared to use a little deception. Whether it's a grand production to fool the an entire audience or a little white lie to smooth things over, even dishonesty has its place.

Howell Davis made deception his specialty. He once captured a heavily-armed French ship by announcing that he outnumbered them two-to-one, when in reality Davis' second ship was a mere merchant trader whose crew he'd forced into pretending to be pirates. In 1719 with fewer than a dozen men he staged an audacious raid on the Royal African Company's fort in Gambia, using disguises to secure an invitation to dinner with the Governor.

"He told them, that there was a great deal of Money always kept in Gambia Castle, and that it would be worth their while to make an Attempt upon it. They ask'd him how it was possible, since it was garrisoned? He desired they would leave the Management of it to him, and he would undertake to make them Masters of it. ... he himself, with the Master and Doctor, dressed themselves like Gentlemen; his Design being, that the Men should look like common Sailors, and they like Merchants. ... Davis on a sudden drew out a Pistol, clapt it to the Governor's Breast, telling him, he must surrender the Fort and all the Riches in it, or he was a dead Man."

25

- Charles Johnson, "A General History of the Pyrates" (1724)

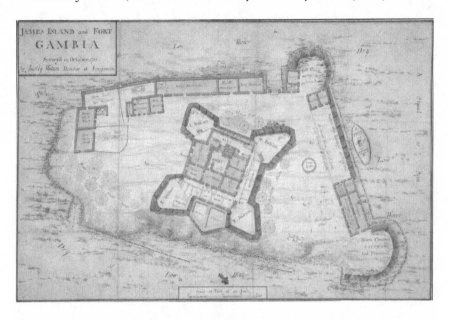

Davis was later killed trying to loot the island of Principe using the same strategy after an escaped slave swam to shore and warned the Governor, who allowed Davis ashore in order to ambush him. Still, trickery had worked so well for this master of deception, it was only reasonable to trust his skills at subterfuge. If he had succeeded, we might still be singing songs about Howell Davis.

A FURTHER VOYAGE

Upon his death in 1719, Davis – described by captured sailor William Snelgrave as "a most generous humane Person" – was replaced as Captain by Bartholomew "Black Bart" Roberts, who would soon become one of the most successful pirates of the Golden Age.

10: A GOOD STORY HELPS

Maybe it's a witty anecdote to break the ice at a party or a deeply personal recollection to prove to someone that you trust them with your secrets. No matter the cause or occasion, stories are a staple of how we communicate and remember as humans. History or fiction, they can calm and inspire and even serve as tools of the trade - even an illicit trade.

In 1699 pirate John James had let Colonial officials think he was a Dutch pirate named Hynd, a ruse that worked until he outfought the elderly and leaking guard-ship *Essex Prize* off Virginia and proceeded to loot merchant shipping in the bay. He questioned the Captain of a merchantman, telling him there was another pirate coming to join him (there wasn't), that he'd already captured fantastic wealth (he hadn't), and finally masquerading as a far more famous pirate before he released his prisoners and sailed away.

"[August 1699] Account by Richard Burgess, Master of the *Maryland Merchant* of Bristol ... [the pirate] ship had on board, as they generally reported themselves, £3,000,000 sterling in gold and silver. They thought it not worth their while to take a gentleman's plate and money, value nigh £100, that was on board [my own ship]. ... He asked me for whom I thought the *Essex Prize* was cruising. I informed, one Capt. Kidd. He answered, 'I am Kidd.' He was called John James by the Company; but from the description I have of him in the country, he is said to be Kidd."

- Cecil Headlam, "Calendar of State Papers Colonial, America and West Indies: Volume 17" (1908)

James' tall tale came at the right time: the real Captain Kidd was arrested the same month in which James interrogated the captured merchant. His fanciful stories threw naval patrols off his trail, kept captured sailors from fighting back, and kept colonial officials from pursuing him too hard. They couldn't save him from wrecking on a reef shortly afterwards, but I'm sure he'd have had a great yarn to spin for the mermaids.

11: DON'T BELIEVE THE HYPE

"If it's too good to be true, it probably is." "Where there's smoke, there's fire." Those are old adages but they still apply: do your research and trust your gut to know what's realistic and what's just "spin."

England's King William III offered a pardon in 1698 to pirates who willingly surrendered. Joseph Bradish and his cohorts had sailed aboard the ship *Adventure* before staging a mutiny and marooning its crew. After selling off the *Adventure's* cargo they turned themselves in and expected to receive the King's Grace. Instead they were arrested, tried, and hanged alongside William Kidd.

"Captain Carey, whose ship was taken by Roberts in April 1720 wrote, 'Whilst I was in the hands of the Pirates nothing was heard from these rascals the whole time but swearing, damning and blaspheming to the last degree imaginable saying they would have no dealings with Acts of Grace, by which to be sent to hang a-sundrying at Hope Point as were the companies of Kidd and Bradish, trepanned under lying promises. If they were attacked by too strong a force they would blow up their ships and all go merrily to hell.' "
- Charles Grey, "Pirates of the Eastern Seas" (1933)

This quote came from a sailor captured by Bartholomew Roberts some twenty years after Bradish and Kidd met their end. Kidd himself had sailed out a legal privateer and returned accused of piracy, a crime he denied all the way to his grave. Two decades later, pirates still held up Bradish and Kidd as examples of Royal promises which really were too good to be believed.

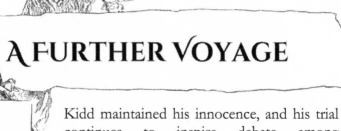

A FURTHER VOYAGE

Kidd maintained his innocence, and his trial continues to inspire debate among researchers and historians. Even if he were innocent of piracy, he was still convicted of killing an argumentative crewman.

12: SOME CIRCUMSTANCES CALL FOR DESPERATE MEASURES

Famous manuals of military strategy since ancient times all counsel something similar: when confronted with a hopeless situation, try something extraordinary! When all else fails and there's nothing left to lose, the time has come to try solutions you might otherwise have thought impossible. Be audacious, and seize the day!

There's a good chance that pirate William Lewis was fictional. Real or not, his story sounds real enough to make for a good example of the most extreme measures. After supposedly serving under real pirate Joseph Bannister, Lewis struck out on his own and raided off Newfoundland in the late 1680s. Sailing across the Atlantic to western Africa, his piratical greed and drive led to the most unusual pact: a deal with Satan himself.

"From Newfoundland he steered for the coast of Guinea, where he took a great many ships, English, Dutch and Portuguese. Among these ships was one belonging to Carolina, commanded by Capt. Smith. While he was in chase of this vessel a circumstance occurred, which made his men believe he dealt with the devil; his fore and main top-mast being carried away, he, Lewis, running up the shrouds to the maintop, tore off a handful of hair, and throwing it into the air used this expression, 'good devil, take this till I come.' And it was observed, that he came afterwards faster up with the chase than before the loss of his top-masts."

- Charles Ellms, "The Pirates Own Book" (1837)

Lewis' black-magic sacrifice may have given his ship *Morning Star* supernatural speed despite loss of its masts, but it was also his undoing. Afterwards, terrified crew and prisoners stabbed him in his cabin as he slept, fearful that he really had sold his soul to infernal powers. Even for a fictional Captain among bloodthirsty cutthroats, there's still such a thing as going too far.

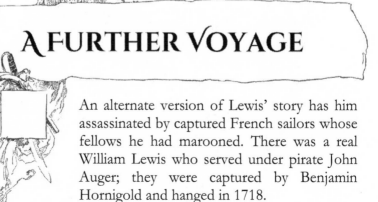

A FURTHER VOYAGE

An alternate version of Lewis' story has him assassinated by captured French sailors whose fellows he had marooned. There was a real William Lewis who served under pirate John Auger; they were captured by Benjamin Hornigold and hanged in 1718.

Matt McLaine

13: SWAGGER COUNTS...

Own the place! There's no impression like a first impression, and nothing leaves a room awestruck like self-confidence. True confidence has the advantage of looking and feeling like it's been earned; an audience can immediately smell the difference between overconfident arrogance and self-assured composure.

The Bahamas were a favorite haunt of Golden Age pirates and the island of New Providence was their chief destination. From 1706 to 1718 the English largely abandoned New Providence, leaving a power vacuum which pirates were quick to exploit. Thomas Barrow declared himself Governor, running roughshod over both the few civilians remaining and the occasional merchant unfortunate enough to put into port in this Republic of Pirates.

"Deposition of John Vickers: ... One Thomas Barrow formerly mate of a Jamaica brigantine which run away some time ago with a Spanish marquiss's money and effects, is the chief of them and gives out that he only waits for a vessell to go out a pirating, that he is Governor of Providence and will make it a second Madagascar, and expects 5 or 600 men more from Jamaica sloops to join in the settling of Providence, and to make war on the French and Spaniards, but for the English, they don't intend to meddle with them, unless they are first attack'd by them ... It is common for the sailors now at Providence (who call themselves the flying gang) to extort money from the inhabitants, and one Capt. Stockdale ... was threatened to be whipp'd for not giving them what they demanded, and just upon his coming from thence he payed them 20sh. for which the aforementioned Barrow and one Peter Parr gave him a receipt on the publick account."

- Cecil Headlam, "Calendar of State Papers Colonial, America and West Indies: Volume 29" (1930)

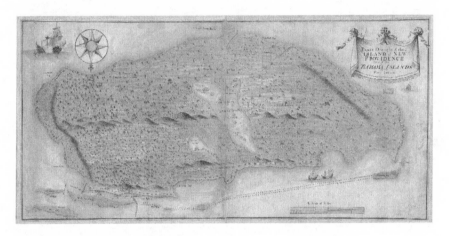

Not only did Barrow declare himself Governor, he went so far as to give people invoices after he'd robbed them! All that swagger paid off: he took the King's Pardon and was living peacefully on the same island years later, no one ever seriously having considered prosecuting the former "Governor."

14: ...AND CHUTZPAH WORKS

Confidence matters, but it counts for far more when you're ready to follow it up with action. Back up your talk with guts and gusto! There's a reason that "who dares, wins" is a saying.

New York hosted a number of successful privateers at the dawn of the 18th century. Among the best-known were Captains Penniston and Gincks, who fought best when outnumbered; Tongrelow, who always chose the largest targets he could see; and Burches, who had no fear whatsoever. Burches once attacked a Spanish galleon which outgunned him 4-to-1 and outmanned him 10-to-1, and humiliated them into giving up their cargo just to get him to go away.

"...but for down-right insolent daring a bit of work done by Captain Nat Burches fairly takes the lead. Burches commanded Tongrelow's tender, a little sloop of 6 guns and 27 men, which in the charge of a reasonably prudent person would have done her fighting with cockboats of somewhere near her own size. But Burches—bless his honest heart!—had not a scrap of prudence in his whole composition: being one of those cutting and slashing captains whose whole scheme of happiness was summed in his burning longing to get at the enemy, and be d____d to him and the number of his guns!"
- Thomas Janvier, "New York Colonial Privateers" (1895)

Penniston was killed when his penchant for taking on two enemies at once caught up with him, while Burches survived his unbelievable encounters only to be lost at sea. He may have lost his life but his bravery will live forever as a synonym for unrivalled daring and fearlessness.

A FURTHER VOYAGE

Janvier continued: "I do verily believe that he was quite capable of laying his absurd sloop abreast of a King's ship, and of blazing away at her with his deadly little pop-gun broadside, and of winding up by boarding her at the head of his twenty-seven men!"

Matt McLaine

15: BEAT THEM AT THEIR OWN GAME

Sometimes you meet a rival (or even a friend!) who just doesn't get the picture. When that happens, the only way to prove your point is to do so in language they can understand. Bring them around to your way of thinking by playing their game: in these cases "winning" isn't the goal, it's communication! Winning it their way helps drive a point home, too.

Robert Plunkett was the chief agent of Britain's Royal Africa Company outpost at Bunce Island off Sierra Leone. When pirate Bartholomew "Black Bart" Roberts appeared in the harbor in 1721, Plunkett earned Roberts' ire by stubbornly refusing to surrender despite being hopelessly outnumbered. His show of defiance nearly got him killed, until he met Roberts face to face.

"[Roberts] upon the first Sight of Plunkett swore at him like any Devil, for His his Irish Impudence in daring to resist him. Old Plunkett, finding he had got into bad Company, fell a-swearing and cursing as fast or faster than Roberts; which made the rest of the Pirates laugh heartily, desiring Roberts to sit down and hold his Peace, for he had no Share in the Pallaver with Plunkett at all. So that by meer Dint of Cursing and Damning, Old Plunkett, as I am told, sav'd his Life."
- William Smith, "A New Voyage to Guinea" (1745)

Roberts was one of the most successful Golden Age pirates, capturing over 400 ships. Plunkett, on the other hand, was one of the few men to defy Roberts successfully, even if he did so by means of a foul mouth and a fiery temper. He was killed the following year in a gunpowder explosion which sadly never gave him a chance to curse his way to freedom.

16: FLAIR AND PANACHE

There's a place for utility and bare functionality, but that's certainly not the way to make an impression. How much better to do your work with style, and what better way than to go overboard and do something outrageous, just because you can?

Benjamin Hornigold was a colorful character who led a varied life: pirated, salvaged the remains of Spain's sunken 1715 treasure fleet, led the "Flying Gang" pirates who ran the Bahamas, turned pirate hunter, and even mentored Edward "Blackbeard" Teach. Apparently he also knew the value and utility of high fashion, and was the sort of pirate not to take more than he needed from a poor passing merchant.

"[Hornigold and his crew] did us no further injury than the taking most of our hats from us, having got drunk the night before, as they told us, and toss'd theirs overboard."
- British Library, "Additional Ms. 39946" (1724, quoted in Peter Earle's 2003 "The Pirate Wars")

Hornigold was eventually deposed by his crew for refusing to attack fellow English ships. After accepting a Royal pardon he became a pirate hunter for newly-arrived Bahamas Governor Woodes Rogers, successfully bringing to justice some of his former associates. Under the Caribbean sun, a good pirate hunter with a good hat made for a fine combination.

PART THREE:

PLANNING AND PREPARATION

17: IF YOU WANT IT DONE RIGHT, DO IT YOURSELF

You know what you want and you know what you need. The more important something is to you, the more crucial it is to have it done right, and done right the first time. There are things you can't do for yourself, but when you can, who better to get things done just the way you like?

His pirate career may have lasted just a few short months, but William Fly at least has the distinction of marking the end of the Golden Age of pirates. He and his crew aboard the stolen ship *Elizabeth* made a few captures in 1726 before being caught, tried, and condemned to death. Even then, Fly went merrily to his end, and taught his executioner a few things about knot-tying along the way.

"He pass'd along to the place of Execution, with a Nosegay in his hand, and making his Complements, where he thought he saw occasion. Arriving there, he nimbly mounted the Stage, and would fain have put on a Smiling Aspect. He reproached the Hangman, for not understanding his Trade, and with his own Hands rectified matters, to render all things more Convenient and Effectual."
- Cotton Mather, "The Vial poured out upon the Sea" (1726)

He didn't have to teach the hangman how to tie a proper noose, but when you want something done right... Before the noose tightened, Fly warned cruel captains not to abuse their sailors, which may cause them to mutiny as Fly had. Even with his dying words he was still telling other people how to do their jobs.

18: KNOW WHAT YOU'RE GETTING INTO

Before you're nose-deep in something completely foreign, flustering, and overwhelming, do your research. Do your due diligence and know exactly what you're setting yourself up for. A little preparation and planning can save plenty of headache and heartache in the future.

Most pirates gain their first ship by theft or trickery; Stede Bonnet was a wealthy landowner who didn't know any better and had his ship *Revenge* built at his own expense. Most pirate crews operate on a "no prey, no pay" basis. Bonnet tried paying his pirates a regular wage. Most pirate captains know how to sail, to navigate, to fight. Bonnet didn't, and he didn't hide it well.

"Bonnet had no knowledge of the sea, and, as will be seen, knew so little of the requirements of a sailor's life that his first experiences resulted only in disaster and misfortune. ... The *Revenge* had not been out from Barbadoes many days before the men discovered his ignorance of nautical affairs, and this discovery engendered a contempt which soon began to display itself openly, and it was only by the influence of his superior courage that Bonnet prevented an open mutiny. ... They had not proceeded far before Thatch perceived that his companion knew nothing of seamanship, and deeming him an unsafe man to be in command of so fine a sloop as the *Revenge*, coolly deposed him."
- Shirley Carter Hughson, "The Carolina Pirates and Colonial Commerce, 1670-1740" (1894)

Apparently having his ship taken from him by bullies and ingrates spurred him to put his newfound knowledge and experience to use: Bonnet eventually took back the *Revenge* from Edward "Blackbeard"

Teach (Thatch) and went on to have a short if successful pirating career. It didn't save him from being caught in 1718 and hanged a year later, but at least he died like a true pirate and not like a forlorn farmer.

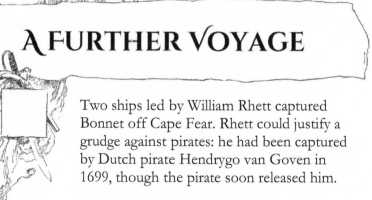

A FURTHER VOYAGE

Two ships led by William Rhett captured Bonnet off Cape Fear. Rhett could justify a grudge against pirates: he had been captured by Dutch pirate Hendrygo van Goven in 1699, though the pirate soon released him.

19: THINK BEFORE YOU ACT

There's a time for decisive action, certainly, but even then it helps to pause for a moment and reflect: am I doing the right thing? Am I going about this the right way? A moment's forethought can reap dividends later. And once you're committed to a course of action, it may be too late for careful plans and cautious review.

David Herriot was going to go free. He had been caught and tried alongside Stede Bonnet in 1718 but agreed to testify against Bonnet to secure a pardon. Despite his certain release, when Bonnet announced his escape plan, he somehow convinced Herriot to accompany him. It wouldn't work out well for either of them.

"[O]n the 24th of October Major Bonnet and Herriot made their Escape ... at last discovering where they were, some of Colonel Rhett's Men fired at them, and killed the Master Herriot upon the Spot ... Nay, not being satisfied with his own Escape, but he must tamper with the King's Evidence, to avoid others being prosecuted and prevailed with the Master Herriot to run away with him, who has been since killed. And I believe the Prisoner at the Bar cannot by reflecting but think himself answerable for that Man's Death."
- South Carolina Court of Vice-Admiralty, "The Tryals of Major Stede Bonnet" (1719)

Bonnet's boatswain Ignatius Pell took the same deal prosecutors had offered Herriot: turn King's Evidence against Bonnet and receive a full pardon. Jailed alongside the other two, he stayed behind when they made their ill-fated getaway. He was pardoned as promised and set free, just as Herriot would have been if he'd taken a moment to think ahead.

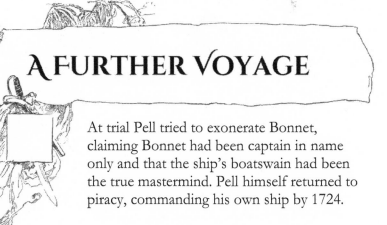

A FURTHER VOYAGE

At trial Pell tried to exonerate Bonnet, claiming Bonnet had been captain in name only and that the ship's boatswain had been the true mastermind. Pell himself returned to piracy, commanding his own ship by 1724.

20: MEAN WHAT YOU SAY

Back up your boasts and keep your promises, and you'll have both admiration and respect. It's not simply a matter of honesty: once you've gained a reputation for untrustworthiness and reneging on promises, it's extremely difficult to clean your name and start over. So begin the right way, by dealing fairly and honestly, and your reputation will precede you.

Many pirates swore they'd rather die than be captured, threatening to blow up their ships if defeat was unavoidable. Stede Bonnet ordered his ship blown up but his men refused; one of Charles Harris' men tried to when they were abandoned by Edward Low but he was prevented, and committed suicide instead; and James Skyrme's men made the attempt but were only burned thanks to their gunpowder supplies being depleted. Joseph Cooper, though, proved he was not a pirate for idle boasts when he was cornered in 1725.

"Skipton, the pirate, with 80 men, is stated to have been taken by his Majesty's ship the *Diamond*, in the bay of Honduras, together with Joseph Cooper, another pirate vessel. When one of these vessels saw he must surrender, the Captain with many of his men went into the cabin and blew themselves up!"
- John F. Watson, "Annals of Philadelphia" (1830)

Bartholomew Roberts' men threatened that "if they were attacked by too strong a force they would blow up their ships and all go merrily to hell," and they certainly tried to - Skyrme was one of his subordinates. Cooper wasn't the only Captain to make good on his threat - an English Royal Navy Captain did so when faced with capture by French buccaneer Etienne de Montauban in 1695 - but Cooper was one of the few pirates to actually pull it off.

21: GET IT IN WRITING

"Trust, but verify." Even between friends, neighbors, and partners, it helps to have everyone on the same page. The best way to be sure there are no surprises in an agreement is to have everything in the open; co-incidentally, it also ensures that for good or ill, everyone's involvement is documented.

Pirate ships operated as something of a democracy, governed by written agreements known as Articles. These pirate "contracts" specified division of plunder, punishments, compensation for injuries, and more. Nicolas Clough's 1683 trial preserved one of the only complete sets of pirate Articles from the 17th century, but he wasn't clear on the part about having his crew sign voluntarily.

"Edward Starkey brought to bar ... Daniel Kelly brought him the writing to sign, Threatening him if he would not. ... Samuel Haywarr, sworn, says ... that the prisoners ordered him to draw the agreement, but he refused, and that John Copping drew them, and he was forced by fear to sign them. ... John Griffin, sworn, says ... He owns to his hand to the writing, but says the master was with his sword in his hands and threatened those that did not sign it. ... Wm. Heath, says ... That Henry Lewin pulled him out of his cabin to sign the agreement, and the master threatened to set them on shore on an uninhabited island if they refused ... Albert Lawson says ... that he was forced to sign the agreement by the master."
- New York Historical Society, "Abstracts of Wills on File in the

Surrogate's Office: City of New York" (1893)

Their foolifh Articles were as follows, *(viz.)*

I. THAT every Man fhall obey his Commander in all Refpects, as if the Ship was his own, and we under Monthly Pay.

II. THAT no Man fhall give or difpofe of the Ship's Provifions, whereby may be given Reafon of Sufpicion that every one hath not an equalShare.

III. THAT no Man fhall open or declare to any Perfon or Perfons what we are, or what Defign we are upon ; the Offender fhall be punifh'd with Death upon the fpot.

IV. THAT no Man fhall go on Shore till the Ship is off the Ground, and in readinefs to put to Sea.

V. THAT every Man fhall keep his Watch Night and Day, and precifely at the Hour of Eight leave of Gaming and Drinking, and every one repair to their refpective Stations.

VI. WHOEVER Offends fhall be punifh'd with Death, or otherwife, as we fhall find proper for our Intereft.

Clough had his men swear a solemn promise: "and as you are all here at present you have taken your corporall oath upon the holy Evangelists to stand one by the other as long as life shall last." Many of his sailors had been forced into piracy; while their signatures on his Articles certainly didn't help Clough, their combined testimony, and Clough's need to get it all on paper, helped almost all of them escape conviction.

22: DO YOUR RESEARCH

It never hurts to stop and ask questions. Be sure you've considered all your options before committing to a risky or rash course of action. "Measure twice, cut once" is the saying, and it applies in every facet of life: be certain of your facts, double-check your plans, and proofread! The time spent will pay off in the end.

The buccaneers who raided Spanish territories in the New World may have preceded the Golden Age of Piracy by a few years, but they were all pirates at heart. After buccaneer leader John Watling died in battle at Arica in 1682, Bartholomew Sharp took command of the raiders and captured two rich Spanish ships off the Central American coast. One of them they looted and let go but soon came to regret it.

"[W]e found in the *San Rosario* 700 pigs [ingots] of plate, which we supposed to be tin ... we left them in the *Rosario*, which we turned away loose into the sea. We took only one pig of the 700 into our ship, thinking to make bullets of it ... Thus we parted with the richest booty we got in the whole voyage through our own ignorance and laziness."
- James Burney, "History of the Buccaneers of America" (1816)

Sharp's men only found out what they'd lost when they returned to English territory and gave the leftover "tin" to a man from Bristol, who recognized it for what it was: unrefined silver, which he promptly sold for £75. That was just a fraction of one ingot, and the corsairs had tossed the other 699 into the Pacific. A little research, a test or two, and they all could have retired.

23: LEARN A USEFUL SKILL

The surest job security is to master a critical skill no one else has, thereby making yourself indispensable. There are certain trades and talent always in demand, and in those cases you need to be either multi-talented or exceedingly good. If you have some exotic expertise, though, you're in! Find what everyone needs but no one bothers to master and you can almost name your own salary.

Joseph Wheeler was a cooper (ship's carpenter and barrel-maker) aboard the *Pelican*, hunting treasure ships in the Red Sea under pirate Captain Robert Colley in the late 1690s. They'd had only minor success when fate intervened to give Wheeler a chance to make his mark. After all, you can't go to sea without fresh water, and if your water-barrels go bad...

"Here a Sickness coming among them, they built Huts ashore; they lost, notwithstanding all their Care and Precaution, their Captain and thirty Men, by the Distemper which they contracted; but it abating, they thought of going to Sea again, but on examining their Water Casks, they found the Hoops all worm eaten and rotten, so that there was no Proceeding, but this Defect was repaired by their Cooper, who was an ingenious Fellow; he ... fitted them up, and made them tight, in acknowledging of which Service, they chose him Captain."
- Charles Johnson, "A General History of the Pyrates, Volume 2."
(1724)

Wheeler and the *Pelican* didn't make the kind of impact in the Red Sea that Thomas Tew or Henry Avery did, but they fared well enough for themselves. After dividing their treasure Wheeler returned to New York, where he was tried for piracy but acquitted. No one knows if he went back to barrel-making, but thanks to his in-demand skills, he could afford to rest.

24: GET TO KNOW THE LOCALS

Whether it's learning the hard way which streets not to walk down alone at night, or trying to find the best seafood restaurant in the city, no one knows better than the locals. So go native! Learn the language and the lingo and find a guide who knows the area by heart. Even better when you're in business together: don't just send a message across the ocean, visit and immerse yourself in the market. You'll learn far more with help than you ever could alone!

The Spanish suffered at the hands of English buccaneers for decades, most famously when Henry Morgan ransacked Panama in 1671. Eventually they countered by offering pardons and paychecks to renegade English commanders, and had notable success pairing English and Spanish Captains together. One such pair cornered an English ship in 1730, whose survivors left a detailed narrative of their ordeal.

"[A]nd near an island called Swan Island, about four o'clock in the afternoon, we discovered two sloops making sail after us. The next morning, one of them, called the *Two Brothers*, came up with us. The vessel was Rhode-Island built, with 18 guns, and about 90 men, mostly Spaniards, and commanded by Captain [Henry] Johnson the pirate, an Englishman, and Pedro Polias, a Spaniard."
 - John Cockburn, "The Unfortunate Englishmen" (1732)

It's possible Cockburn's memoir was wholly or partially fictional, but even if so, Johnson and Polias were hardly the only English / Spanish co-Captains in the Golden Age of Piracy. Richard Noland sharing command with Don Benito, Richard Hancock serving alongside Augustin Blanco, Polias and Johnson - all were successful, at least in part because they could cooperate to command their ships with the best of both worlds.

PART FOUR:

A CERTAIN *JE NE SE QUOI*

25: PERSEVERE THROUGH IT ALL

Sometimes things get rough and there's no quick or easy solution; in times like those, the only thing to do is keep your chin up and tough it out. It takes an iron will to endure the worst life can throw at you and nerves of steel to keep enduring day after day. Just as important, if not more so, is to keep up hope. Losing hope makes all the effort and fortitude pointless; with it, you can outlast any troubles.

Among the cruelest pirates of the Golden Age was Edward Low, who captured and forced sailor Philip Ashton into service in 1722. Ashton escaped when the pirates stopped at the island of Roatán near Honduras. Marooned alone with no tools or weapons, evading pirates and Spanish soldiers, he survived for a year and a half before he was rescued.

"Two Years, Ten Months and Fifteen Days, after I was first taken by the Pirate Low; and Two Years, and near two Months after I had made my Escape from him upon Roatan Island. I went the same Evening to my Father's House, where I was received, as one coming to them from the Dead, with all Imaginable Surprise of Joy."
- John Barnard, "Ashton's Memorial" (1725)

Ashton's Memorial.

A N
H I S T O R Y
O F T H E
Strange Adventures,
A N D
Signal Deliverances,
O F
Mr. *Philip Ashton,*

Who, after he had made his Escape from the
PIRATES, liv'd alone on a Desolate
Island for about Sixteen Months, &c.

W I T H

A short Account of Mr. *Nicholas Merritt,*
who was taken at the same time.

To which is added

A *SERMON* on *Dan.* 3. 17.

By JOHN BARNARD, V. D. M.

—— *We should not trust in our selves, but in God;*
—— *who delivered us from so great a Death, and doth
deliver; in whom we trust, that he will yet deliver us.*
II. Cor. I. 9, 10.

BOSTON, N. E. Printed for *Samuel Gerrish,*
at his Shop in Corn-Hill, 1 7 2 5.

Together with the tale of Alexander Selkirk (whose marooning inspired Defoe to write *Robinson Crusoe*), Ashton's torments became a model for stories of castaways and survival against the odds. His faith, determination, and willpower carried him through an unbelievable trial. His captors were hunted down and never lived to enjoy their stolen wealth, while Ashton calmly returned to his life on the sea.

A FURTHER VOYAGE

Selkirk's tale inspired Daniel Defoe to write *Robinson Crusoe* in 1719; Ashton's ordeal may have inspired Defoe to write *The Four Years Voyages of Capt. George Roberts* in 1726. Many historians doubt Defoe actually wrote it, but Roberts' tale does strongly parallel Ashton's.

Matt McLaine

26: KNOW WHEN TO QUIT

Ever get the feeling you should stop while you're ahead? It might be time to trust your gut - "get out while the gettin's good," as they say. Don't get carried away by greed or fanaticism. Once you've met your goal, or come as close to it as is reasonable, then it's time to think long and hard about diminishing rewards versus increasing risk and effort to achieve them. Know when enough is enough.

They called it the Pirate Round - sailing from New England, around Africa at the Cape of Good Hope, a stop at Madagascar to refit and resupply, then into the Indian Ocean or Persian Gulf to raid the rich treasure ships. Thomas Tew pioneered the route for pirates in 1692, returning fantastically rich for little risk. He tried to retire, but fame and a restless crew wouldn't let him rest.

"Captain Tew lived unquestioned in America for some time, having an easy fortune and designing to live quietly. But some of the old Company who lived near him having squandered their shares continually desired him to make a new voyage. He withstood them for some time, until they, having got together by spreading reports of the vast riches to be obtained, a number of resolute fellows, at last induced him to head them for a last voyage. They prepared a small ship and making the best of their way to the Red Sea, entered the straights of Bal-el-Mandeb where they met with and attacked a ship belonging to the Great Mogull. In the engagement a great shot carried away the rim of Tew's belly who held in his bowels for a small

space until he dropped, which spread such terror amongst his men that they suffered themselves to be taken without resistance."
- Charles Grey, "Pirates of the Eastern Seas" (1933)

The other ships he'd met with en route went on to participate in Henry Every's attack on the Gunsway, one of the richest pirate captures of all time. And Tew's men, led by his quartermaster John Ireland, went on to other piratical adventures without him. Tew was set for life, had been wined and dined by Governors, and should have stayed home. Henry Every did: after his final raid, he changed his name and slipped quietly into obscurity.

27: NEVER TOO LATE FOR REDEMPTION

Some sins are harder to atone for than others, but "difficult" doesn't mean "impossible." A life of barbarity can't always be made right overnight, nor can the most horrible of crimes be completely erased by a few good deeds. Still, in the end, the effort does count: sincere repentance, a desire to live a decent life, and genuine hard work toward bravery and kindness in a good cause can go a long way to balancing the scales.

An Ex-Royal Navy sailor, Thomas Pound slipped into local piracy after stealing a small vessel off Massachusetts and kidnapping Captain Thomas Hawkins into semi-willing collaboration. After a tentative start they plundered nearby ships until a pirate-hunting sloop out of Boston brought them to justice. Condemned to die and sent back to England, Pound redeemed himself when given a taste of his own medicine.

"Captain Thomas Pound, pilot and sailing master on the *Rose* frigate; embarked from Boston in Hawkins' boat; wounded in the fight at Tarpaulin Cove, shot in the side and arm and several bones taken out; found guilty but reprieved; sent to England where the charge was dismissed; given command of a ship, and died in 1703 in England, honored and respected."
- George Francis Dow, "The Pirates of the New England Coast, 1630-1730" (1923)

On the way back to England the *Rose* was attacked by a French privateer. Pound was released from his irons and fought so bravely in defense of the *Rose* that he earned the pardon he was given on arrival. He later became a cartographer and navigator whose charts of the New England coast would be unequalled for decades. Hawkins too fought in defense of the *Rose*, and died in the effort; his own pardon had been given before they left.

28: ENJOY WHAT YOU'VE EARNED

You fought the fight and survived, you ran the race and won. Now it's time to bask in your success. You've earned your reward - enjoy it! All work and no play makes for a stressful life, and a life of stress lived without end is a life lived in toil, a life wasted. Take time to smell the roses, and make sure there's a restful goal at the end of your work.

Edward Congdon (often "Christopher Condent" in later stories) had success as one of the late pirates of the Golden Age, capturing ships and valuable cargo from the Caribbean to the Indian Ocean. After capturing a fabulously wealthy Mughal ship in 1720, he and his crew decided that settling down was looking better and better all the time.

"Having now gathered a vast fortune, they thought it time to give up piracy, so they returned to the Island of St. Mary, where they made a share of their plunder, and the company broke up, many of them settling down amongst the natives. Captain Condent and some others sent from here a petition to the Governor of Mauritius asking for a pardon, and received answer that he would take them into his protection if they would destroy their ships. Having done this, they sailed to Mauritius, where they settled down, and Captain Condent married the Governor's sister-in-law. A few years later the captain and his wife left the island and sailed to France, settling at St. Malo, where Condent drove a considerable trade as a merchant."
- Philip Gosse, "The Pirates' Who's Who" (1924)

THE

HISTORY

OF THE

PYRATES,

Containing the LIVES of

Captain *Miſſon*.	Captain *Fly*.
Captain *Bowen*.	Captain *Howard*.
Captain *Kidd*.	Captain *Lewis*.
Captain *Tew*.	Captain *Cornelius*,
Captain *Halſey*.	Captain *Williams*.
Captain *White*.	Captain *Burgeſs*.
Captain *Condent*.	Captain *North*.
Captain *Bellamy*.	

And their ſeveral C R E W S.

Intermix'd with a

Deſcription of M A G A D O X A in *Ethiopia*; the natural Hatred and Cruelty of the Inhabitants to all Whites; their Laws, Manners, Cuſtoms, Government and Religion: With a particular ACCOUNT of the beautiful Tombs, and their Ceremony of guarding them, taken from Captain *Beavis*'s Journal; and that of a Molotto, who belong'd to the ſaid Captain, was taken by, and lived ſeveral Years with the MAGADOXIANS.

To the Whole is added

An APPENDIX, which compleats the Lives of the firſt Volume, corrects ſome Miſtakes; and contains the Tryal and Execution of the Pyrates at *Providence*; under Governor *Rogers*; with ſome other neceſſary Inſertions, which did not come to Hand till after the Publication of the firſt Volume, and which makes up what was defective. Collected from Journals of Pyrates, brought away by a Perſon who was taken by, and forc'd to live with them 12 Years; and from thoſe of Commanders, who had fallen into their Hands, ſome of whom have permitted their Names to be made uſe of, as a Proof of the Veracity of what we have publiſhed. The Whole inſtructive and entertaining.

V O L. II.

By Capt. CHARLES JOHNSON, Author of Vol. I.

Omne tulit punctum, qui miſcuit utile dulci. Hor.

L O N D O N:

Printed for, and Sold by T. WOODWARD, at the *Half-moon*, over-againſt St. *Dunſtan*'s Church, *Fleet-ſtreet*.

Comparatively few pirates survived to retire, and fewer of them still did so with their riches intact. Henry Every disappeared into the Irish countryside with his riches, Henry Jennings retired to plantation life, William May ran a tavern which still exists today - all of them lived to enjoy the good life, though few had as long and prosperous a retirement as Congdon.

A FURTHER VOYAGE

A few pirates retired not just rich, but to genuine respectability: George Dew became a lawyer and Assembly member on Bermuda, while Josiah Burgess returned to Nassau and became a Justice on the Vice-Admiralty court.

29: KARMA'S A BITCH

What goes around, comes around! Spiritually-minded persons might describe heaven or hell awaiting us, or a cycle of reincarnation to work off our transgressions. On the worldly side there's always prison. But sometimes retribution for a life of violence and debauchery comes in a far more immediate form, by which time it's probably too late to make amends and treat others fairly and kindly.

When John Phillips took the sloop *Squirrel* from Andrew Harradine, he made the mistake of keeping the disgruntled sailing master aboard. Pirates often forced talented sailors to join their crews, and Phillips had done so more than once. He learned too late that you can only kick a dog just so many times before it decides to bite back.

"Harradine struck down Phillips the Captain with an adds [adze], and another man struck Burrell the Boatswain with a Broad Ax; and the rest fell upon James Sparks the Gunner, and having in a few Minutes dispatched the said Four Officers, the rest of the Pirates immediately surrendered themselves Prisoners."
- Massachusetts Historical Society Collection vol. XLVII, quoted in John Franklin Jameson, "Privateering and Piracy in the Colonial Period" (1923)

The ax-wielding sailor who sided with Harradine was John Fillmore, great-grandfather of future U.S. President Millard Fillmore, and had been forced aboard as well. Other forced men rose up against pirates like William Fly, John Fenn, and James Fife. Phillips was among the last of the Golden Age pirates, and his death marked the end of an era - though not the end of piracy.

30: CLEANLINESS IS NEXT TO GODLINESS

There's really no excuse for living in filth and squalor. Understandably there can be higher priorities than sweeping up, and when recycling isn't easy or fast, it falls even further down the list. Further still, when you do have time and resources to devote to cleaning up, and simply choose not to, it can lead to health dangers and worse.

In his home in Genoa he might have been called Matteo Luco, but in service to Spain the English called him Matthew Luke. The Spanish were never squeamish about letting foreigners command their Coast Guard ships (a polite term for their anti-English privateers), and in Matthew Luke they had a successful ally. They could have chosen better, though: a mere scrap of paper taken from one of his victims was his undoing.

"About the same Time, a Guard le Coast, of Porto Rico, commanded by one Matthew Luke, an Italian, took four English Vessels, and murthered all the Crews: He was taken by the *Lanceston* Man of War, in May 1722, and brought to Jamaica, were they were all but seven deservedly hanged. ... Afterwards in rummaging there was found a Cartridge of Powder made up with a Piece of an English Journal, belonging, I believe, to the *Crean* Snow; and upon Examination, at last, it was discovered that they had taken this Vessel and murthered the Crew; and one of the Spaniards, when he came to die, confessed that he had killed twenty English Men with his own Hands."

- Charles Johnson, "A General History of the Pyrates" (1724)

A Spanish Guarda Costa boarding Capt. Jenkins's Ship and Cutting off his Ear.

Maybe the lesson should have been "be more careful about how and what you recycle" but it wouldn't have helped Luke's case. The Spanish protested that he had a legitimate privateering commission but he and his crew were hanged nonetheless. His ship may have been named *Venganza*, but it was the *Crean's* dead sailors who finally had their own vengeance thanks to a scrap of paper.

31: VARIETY IS THE SPICE OF LIFE

Drudgery and routine can sap the life from anyone. Mix it up a little! Even if you don't stray far from your comfort zone, a change of scenery can work wonders for cultivating a healthy mental state. Whether it's learning a new fact every day or trying a new restaurant every month, those little variations keep things fresh and fun.

Few pirate ships were completely crewed by sailors from a single nation. Even on the staunchest English vessel there were almost always a few Irishmen or the occasional Frenchman. Some ships, though, went all-out with completely mixed-race and mixed-nationality crews and had great success to show for it.

"Deposition of John Bois, Carpenter of the *Wade* frigate, — Edwards Commander. Antigua, Feb. 24th, 1719. ... The pirates had on board about 130 white men, and about 50 Spaniards, negroes and Indians, 26 guns and 4 swivel guns, commanded by Edward England an Irishman."
"Deposition of Robert Leathes, Commander of the *Upton* pink of Belfast. Antigua, 12th March, 1719. On 17th Jan. he was taken by a pirate brigantine, Richard Frowd Commander, in latitude 35 North, in his voyage from Belfast to South Carolina. The brigantine had about 4 guns and 60 men whites and blacks, and was tender to the pirate ship *Rising Sun*."
"Deposition of John Brown, late Commander of the brigantine *John and Thomas* of Road Island. Antigua, 12th March, 1719. On Nov. 5th

last he was taken off the Bay of Carolina by a pirate ship, the *Rising Sun*, William Moudy Commander, mounted with 36 guns and having on board 130 men, white and black."

"Capt. Vernon, Commander in Chief of H.M. ships at Jamaica, to Mr. Burchett. 8th March, 1720. ... Simon Mascarino a Portuguese and noted villain in these parts where he has been privatier and pirate above 20 years. ... He was going to St. Domingo to complete his crew, not for trading, but privateering off the coast of Jamaica. His crew was made up of all nations and colours."

- Cecil Headlam, "Calendar of State Papers Colonial, America and West Indies: Volume 30" (1930) and "Volume 32" (1933)

It didn't always work out in the end, of course. Hendrygo "Hind" van Goven had a mixed crew of French, English, Dutch, and other sailors and was feared enough to earn the name "The Grand Pyrate Hynde." Disgruntled Englishmen led by John James staged a mutiny, took over his ship, and marooned the others. Even variety has its price: ill treatment and lack of common goals turned diversity into disaster for Hind.

32: BE MAGNANIMOUS

Whether it's karma or conscience, sometimes the right thing is the only thing we can do. They say character is who we are in the dark: it's how we treat others when there's no reward in it for us that matters. A little generosity can go a long way, even (or especially) when the only benefit we can see from it is a peaceful heart and a mind put at ease.

When apprehended and put on trial, most pirates resorted to claiming they'd been captured and forced into piracy. By the 1700s Colonial judges and juries were beginning to tire of piracy and this defense was often ignored. Sometimes, though, it happened to be true. One pirate Captain named Lodowick (or Lewis) Ferdinando regretted forcing men to join him and wrote a unique letter for a captured sailor named Briggs.

"I Captain Lodowick Ferdinando, do hereby solemnly protest and declare, in the presence of Capt. Benjin Joyce, Master of the *John and Jane*, and Wm White, Mr of the *Unity*, that James Briggs now aboard of Capt. Joyce, was forced by me against his will from on Board the *Resolution*, Captain Humphry Ware Commander. And now finding it uneasy, to carry men unwilling to my service, I have therefore both in pitty and generosity, dismissed the said James Briggs and declare him an unfaithfull servant to me but willing every way, as well as Capable, to serve any Merchant Man whatsoever, Therefore I hope these my Letters, shall never tend to his prejudice. In presence of the said

Witnesses I have both signed and subscribed the same. - Lodowick Ferdinando"
- The National Archives of England, State Papers, "Certificate of James Briggs" (1700, quoted in E. T. Fox's 2014 "Pirates in Their Own Words")

Ferdinando had looted a number of ships in quick succession in 1700; Briggs was later arrested and accused of assisting the pirates, but Ferdinando's letter saved him. Bermuda's Governor Benjamin Bennett generously sent a number of bounty-hunting privateers after Ferdinando, but being the unselfish pirate that he was, he politely declined to be captured.

BIBLIOGRAPHY

The following works are quoted liberally throughout this book. These early writings generally do not cite their sources or give credit to a story's first appearance. Where possible I quoted only passages which were borne out by more modern research or which have been generally accepted as accurate. All but a few of these are in the public domain and many are freely available online.

Barnard, John. "Ashton's memorial. An history of the strange adventures, and signal deliverances, of Mr. Philip Ashton." Boston: Samuel Gerrish, 1725.

British Library. "Additional Manuscripts 39946: 'NARRATIVE of voyages to the Guinea Coast and the West Indies, 1713/4-1716, followed by items of West Indian news from Barbados, 1722-1723/4'". British Library, 1724. (Quoted in Earle, Peter. "The Pirate Wars." New York: St. Martin's Press, 2003.)

Burney, James, F.R.S. "History of the Buccaneers of America." London: Payne and Foss, 1816.

Cockburn, John. "The Unfortunate Englishmen" Edinburgh: Waugh & Innes, 1735.

Dow, George Francis, and John Henry Edmonds. "The Pirates of the New England Coast, 1630-1730." Salem: Marine Research Society, 1923.

Earle, Peter. "The Pirate Wars." London: Methuen, 2003.

Ellms, Charles. "The Pirates Own Book, Or Authentic Narratives of the Lives, Exploits, and Executions of the Most Celebrated Sea Robbers." Portland: Sanborn & Carter, 1837.

Fortescue, J. W., Ed. "Calendar of State Papers Colonial, America and West Indies: Volume 12 1685-1688 and Addenda 1653-1687." London: Her Majesty's Stationery Office, 1899.

Fox, E. T. "Pirates in Their Own Words." Morrisville NC: Lulu Press, 2014.

Headlam, Cecil, Ed. "Calendar of State Papers Colonial, America and West Indies: Volume 17, 1699 and Addenda 1621-1698." London: His Majesty's Stationery Office, 1908.

Headlam, Cecil, Ed. "Calendar of State Papers Colonial, America and West Indies: Volume 30, 1717-1718." London: His Majesty's Stationery Office, 1930.

Headlam, Cecil, Ed. "Calendar of State Papers Colonial, America and West Indies: Volume 32, 1717-1718." London: His Majesty's Stationery Office, 1933.

Gosse, Philip. "The Pirates' Who's Who: Giving Particulars Of The Lives and Deaths Of The Pirates And Buccaneers." New York: Burt Franklin, 1924.

Grey, Charles. "Pirates of the Eastern Seas." London: Sampson Low, Marston & Co., Ltd., 1933.

Hughson, Shirley Carter. "The Carolina Pirates and Colonial Commerce, 1670-1710" in "Johns Hopkins University Studies in Historical and Political Science," Volume XII. Baltimore: Johns Hopkins University Press, 1894.

Jameson, John Franklin. "Privateering and Piracy in the Colonial Period: Illustrative Documents." New York: The Macmillan Company, 1923.

Johnson, Charles. "A General History of the Pyrates: from their first rise and settlement in the island of Providence, to the present time." London: T. Warner, 1724.

Johnson, Charles. "The History of the Pyrates, Vol. II." London: T. Warner, 1728.

Janvier, Thomas. "New York Colonial Privateers" in "Harper's New Monthly Magazine", Volume XC, February 1895. New York: Harper & Brothers Publishers, 1895.

Mather, Cotton. "The vial poured out upon the sea. A remarkable relation of certain pirates brought unto a tragical and untimely end. Some conferences with them, after their condemnation. Their behaviour at their execution. And a sermon preached on that occasion." Boston: T. Fleet, 1726.

National Archives of England (The), State Papers 34/ 14/ 15a, f. 19. "Certificate of James Briggs." Reprinted with permission from Fox, E.T. "Pirates In Their Own Words." Durham: Lulu Press, 2014.

New York Historical Society. "Abstracts of Wills on File in the Surrogate's Office: City of New York, Volume 1, 1667-1707" New York: New York Historical Society, 1893.

Smith, William. "A new voyage to Guinea: describing the customs, manners, soil, manual arts, agriculture, trade, employments, languages, ranks of distinction climate, habits, buildings, education, habitations, diversions, marriages, and whatever else is memorable among the inhabitants." London: John Nourse, 1745.

Snow, Edward Rowe. "Pirates and Buccaneers of the Atlantic Coast." Boston: The Yankee Publishing Co., 1944.

South Carolina Court of Vice-Admiralty. "The Tryals of Major Stede Bonnet and Other Pirates." London: Benjamin Cowse, 1719.

Watson, John F., and Willis P. Hazard, Eds. "Annals of Philadelphia, and Pennsylvania, in the olden time; being a collection of memoirs, anecdotes, and incidents of the city and its inhabitants, and of the earliest settlements of the inland part of Pennsylvania." Philadelphia: Edwin S. Stuart, 1884.

IMAGE CREDITS

All images used in this work are freely available online and are believed to be in the public domain.

Cover: "Dance of the Pirates" by William Russell Flint, from the libretto of Gilbert and Sullivan's "Savoy Operas" (1909).

Dedication: Interior art by Howard Pyle, from "Howard Pyle's Book of Pirates" (1921).

Preface: "New York as it Appeared about 1690" by Howard Pyle, from "The Sea Robbers of New York" by Thomas Janvier (1894).

Further Voyage notes: Adapted from interior art by Howard Pyle, from "New York Colonial Privateers" by Thomas Janvier (1895).

Chapter 1: "French Man-of-War, ca. 1700", by anonymous, from the National Maritime Museum, Greenwich, London (1700).

Chapter 2: "Captain Halsey, The Dutchman Acquainted them of their Error" from Pirates of the Spanish Main series for Allen & Ginter Cigarettes (1888).

Chapter 3: "Captain Snelgrave and the Pirates" from "The True Story Book" by Andrew Lang (1893).

Chapter 4: "A Pirate hanged at Execution Dock" by Robert Dodd, from the National Maritime Museum, Greenwich, London (1795).

Chapter 5: "Woodes Rogers, former Pirate, Governor of the Bahamas" by William Hogarth (1729).

Chapter 6: "Vane arrested by Captain Holford" from "The Pirates Own Book" by Charles Ellms (1837).

Chapter 7: "She Would Sit Quite Still, Permitting Barnaby to Gaze" by Howard Pyle (1896).

Chapter 8: "He Had Found the Captain Agreeable and Companionable" by Howard Pyle (1894).

Chapter 9: "James Island and Fort Gambia" by Justly Watson (1755).

Chapter 10: Anonymous, painting of a pirate ship, possible copy of Ambroise-Louis Garneray's "La Prise du Kent par Surcouf" (1852).

Chapter 11: "Captain Kidd hanging in chains" from "The Pirates Own Book" by Charles Ellms (1837).

Chapter 12: "Captain Lewis giving a lock of his hair to the Devil" from "The Pirates Own Book" by Charles Ellms (1837).

Chapter 13: "Exact Draught of the Island of New Providence, One of the Bahama Islands in the West Indies," US Library of Congress (circa 1700-1750).

Chapter 14: "AND AGAIN MY CAPTAIN TOOK THE BIGGEST" by Howard Pyle (1895).

Chapter 15: "Captain Roberts' Crew carousing at Old Calabar River" from "The Pirates Own Book" by Charles Ellms (1837).

Chapter 16: Interior illustration, anonymous, from "A General History of the Pyrates" by Charles Johnson (1724).

Chapter 17: "Cottonus Matherus S." by Peter Pelham (circa 1700).

Chapter 18: "The Hanging of Major Stede Bonnet," anonymous, from "A General History of the Pyrates" by Charles Johnson (1725).

Chapter 19: "Colonel Rhett and the pirate" by Howard Pyle (1921).

Chapter 20: "The Burning Ship" by Howard Pyle (1911).

Chapter 21: From "An account of the conduct and proceedings of the late John Gow," attributed to Daniel Defoe (1725).

Chapter 22: "An Attack on a Galleon" by Howard Pyle (1905).

Chapter 23: "The Cooper" ("De Kupier") by Jan Luyken (1694).

Chapter 24: Frontispiece illustration from "The unfortunate Englishmen; or, A faithful narrative of the distresses and adventures of John Cockburn" (1831).

Chapter 25: Title page of "Ashton's memorial. An history of the strange adventures, and signal deliverances, of Mr. Philip Ashton" (1725).

Chapter 26: "Captain Tew attacks the ship from India" from "The Pirates Own Book" by Charles Ellms (1837).

Chapter 27: "A new mapp of New England" by Thomas Pound, courtesy of the Norman B. Leventhal Map & Education Center at the Boston Public Library (1691).

Chapter 28: Title page from "The History of the Pyrates" by Charles Johnson (or "A General History of the Pyrates, Vol. 2" (1725).

Chapter 29: US President Millard Fillmore, photograph by Mathew B. Brady, from the U.S. Library of Congress (circa 1855-1865).

Chapter 30: "A Spanish Guarda Costa boarding Captain Jenkin's Ship and Cutting Off His Ear" by anonymous, (1731).

Chapter 31: "Pour, oh pour the pirate sherry" by William Russell Flint, from the libretto of Gilbert and Sullivan's "Savoy Operas" (1909).

Chapter 32: "Avary Sells His Jewels" by Howard Pyle (1887).

About the Author: Interior art by Howard Pyle, from "Howard Pyle's Book of Pirates," 1921.

ABOUT THE AUTHOR

Matt McLaine is the son of loving parents, husband of a wonderful wife, father of a delightful daughter, and companion of two cats and two retired racing greyhounds. He lives in the South Carolina Lowcountry, less than an hour from where pirates Richard Worley and John Cole once lurked off Charles Towne harbor, and has fished the same Edisto River where Charles Yeats once anchored his ship while waiting for a pardon from the Governor.

Made in the USA
Lexington, KY
22 February 2019